A FOOTE

DALVIN COOK

by

Doug Olson, Jr.

LAKE 7 CREATIVE LLC

Minneapolis, Minnesota

Dedication
For Jeff King. Because some of the greatest coaches don't lead a professional sports team or make national headlines.

Edited by Jennifer Mitchell and Ryan Jacobson.
Fact-checked by Natalie Fowler.
Cover design by Ryan Jacobson.

Published by Lake 7 Creative, LLC
Minneapolis, MN 55412
www.lake7creative.com

Printed in the USA.

ISBN: 978-1-940647-49-4
eISBN: 978-1-940647-50-0

TABLE OF CONTENTS

1

CHASE

Dalvin Cook was born in Miami, Florida, on August 10, 1995. His parents were James Cook and Varondria Burnett. Dalvin had two brothers, James and DeAndre; and three sisters, Daniesha, Jamiya, and Jameisha.

As a young child, Dalvin's favorite game was "chase." The kids simply ran around, trying to catch each other. Dalvin always got bored after a few rounds. Nobody could catch him.

It didn't take long for Dalvin's love of "chase" to morph into a love of football. At age four, he began playing in the Florida Youth Football League for the Scott Lake Vikings. He was bigger and faster than most of the other participants, so he played as a linebacker on defense. His job was to stop the quarterbacks and running backs from gaining yards or scoring touchdowns.

As the years passed, Dalvin kept getting stronger—and kept getting faster. When he was just 10 years old, he caught the attention of Larry Blustein, a local recruiting analyst. Blustein tagged Dalvin as a potential superstar and noted his incredible speed.

At age 12, Dalvin became a running back on offense. His new job was to carry the football and score touchdowns—and he scored a lot of touchdowns for the Pee Wee Carol City Chiefs.

When he reached middle school, Dalvin felt uncertain about the local high school, Carol City High. He wasn't sure that the football program could teach him enough or challenge him enough to reach his goal of playing football in college. He wanted to attend Miami Central High, a football powerhouse.

When he was 13 years old, Dalvin made a very important change in his life. He asked to live with his Grandma Betty in Ocka-Locka, Florida. The woman whom Dalvin affectionately called "Ma" did not ask why and did not ask for how long. She simply said yes. So Dalvin moved in with Ma

Dalvin began playing football when he was four years old.

and her son, Anthony Jones, who was a few years younger than Dalvin. His new neighborhood was only 10 miles south of where he grew up, and he visited his mother often.

Dalvin's grandmother was a positive influence on the boys' lives, but she couldn't always keep them safe and out of trouble. In 2009, when Dalvin was 14 years old, he was reportedly arrested and charged with robbery. The charges were later dropped.

A year later, as a freshman, he was reportedly charged with possessing and firing a weapon on school property. Nothing ever came of those charges either.

He didn't get a chance to make his mark with Miami Central that year. The team already had a star running back: Devonta Freeman. But Freeman was a senior; he'd be moving on to college. Dalvin would get his chance to shine the following year.

Football eased Dalvin's transition into his new school. Despite a quiet nature, Dalvin gained the attention of several classmates, teachers, and coaches who saw his playmaking ability.

He made friends—a lot of them. Boys began to gather at Grandma Betty's house after school and after football practice. She cared greatly for Dalvin's friends. She made peanut butter and jelly sandwiches every day, Monday through Thursday, for Dalvin to share with his teammates.

Before long, Tavius Brown, a wide receiver for the team, moved into the home of "Miss Betty," as she was affectionately called. Another player, Da'Vante Phillips, spent so much time at the house that Miss Betty felt he lived there too.

For his part, Dalvin began making better choices and staying out of trouble. As Miss Betty put it, "He was doing wild, crazy things in middle school, but he straightened up at the high school."

2

TWO RUNNING BACKS

Under coach Telly Lockette, Dalvin played on offense and defense his sophomore year. He served as a defensive back, and he shared running back duties with Joseph Yearby. The two quickly became best friends.

The duo took turns as the team's featured running back. During any given game, whoever seemed to be doing better got the most carries. Sometimes it was Dalvin. Other times it was Yearby. On some plays, the team lined up in a "wildcat" formation. On these plays, Yearby became the quarterback, and he could either run the ball or hand it off to Dalvin.

Fans, friends, and family members soon found themselves debating who was the better running back. Some people didn't want the two boys to be friends. They believed the running backs would become even better players if they worked against each other.

Yet their friendship pushed them further and brought them more success than any rivalry could. They spent time working out together, playing video games—and winning a lot of football games. They talked about their futures. They both wanted to win college championships, and they both wanted to win college football's Heisman Memorial Trophy, awarded to the best football player in the National Collegiate Athletic Association (NCAA).

Early during the 2011 season, Dalvin tore the rotator cuff in his right shoulder. His doctor told him to quit football for the year because he needed to have surgery.

Dalvin refused. He promised to take care of the shoulder all season and to have surgery as soon as the season ended.

He did his best to keep his promise—all the way to Florida's Class 6A state championship game. Against the Armwood Hawks on December 16, Dalvin shined. He broke off an 80-yard run early in the game and added a 99-yard score on special teams too.

Joe Robbins of *Sports Illustrated* wrote, "In that moment, shoulder screaming, surgery looming, Cook knew: He was going to be great."

Dalvin's efforts were not enough. Armwood came out on top, 40–31, ending the Rockets' dream of a perfect season. Central finished the year at 13–1.

Yearby became the first sophomore in Miami-Dade County to rack up more than 2,000 yards in one season. He finished with 2,160 yards and scored 24 touchdowns. Dalvin finished just shy of 1,000 yards and scored nine touchdowns.

Recruiting analysts Larry Blustein and Jamie Newberg considered them two of Florida's best high school running backs ever.

Months later, it was revealed that Central's quarterback had not been eligible to play. His transfer to the school had violated state rules. The team was forced to forfeit all of their games from the 2011 season. The 13–1 record became 0–14.

3

CHAMPIONSHIP RUN

Dalvin attended the Heath Evans 7-on-7 Flag Football Tournament in June 2012. Named after former National Football League (NFL) fullback Heath Evans, the tournament was an invitation-only event that spotlighted rising high school stars in Florida. It was a good way for colleges to look at the talent they hoped to recruit to their teams.

Dalvin stood out as one of the top players at the event. Recruiters took notice. Many of the nation's best college teams—including Clemson University, the University of Florida, Louisiana State University (LSU), the University of Southern California (USC), and Florida State University (FSU)—all wanted him.

After a meeting with Clemson's head football coach, Dabo Swinney, Dalvin committed to that team. It was perhaps too soon, but Dalvin was excited about the idea of playing football in college. He made a quick decision, even though he still had two years of high school to go.

During the 2012 season, the Central Rockets went 12–1 and played their way into a third straight championship game.

On December 15, they met the Gainesville Hurricanes at Orlando's Camping World Stadium, the home of college football's Citrus Bowl.

Dalvin got his team off to a quick start. On the Rockets' first drive, he caught a short pass in the backfield, turned upfield, and raced 48 yards down the sideline before getting shoved out of bounds at the three-yard line. The explosive play resulted in a field goal.

Yearby added a touchdown later in the quarter, helping Central jump to a 13–7 lead.

In the second quarter, Dalvin scored on a one-yard run, and Yearby added a 19-yard score. The Rockets found their winning formula: Give the ball to Yearby, then Dalvin, then Yearby, then Dalvin.

Central was threatening to score again early in the third quarter. From the six-yard line, Dalvin took the football and headed to his left. He ran into a pair of defenders, bounced off them, went right, and raced to the corner of the end zone for a score.

Gainesville managed a touchdown early in the fourth quarter, and Central added a field goal to their total. Dalvin and his team won a decisive 37–14 victory and were crowned 6A champions.

Dalvin finished the season with 132 carries for 1,451 yards, along with 269 yards receiving. He scored 22 rushing touchdowns and two receiving touchdowns. Yearby gained 1,448 yards on 212 attempts, with 20 touchdowns. He also caught a touchdown pass.

After his successful year, Dalvin was considered a top running back in the nation. He was ranked as high as third best by 247 Sports.

Although Dalvin had chosen Clemson, other colleges continued to pursue him. In April 2013, Dalvin changed his mind. He switched his college commitment from Clemson to the University of Florida. The Gators were a run-heavy team and would put the ball in his hands often.

In a 247 Sports interview, the young running back assured everyone that his choice was final. "I'm a Gator," he said. "That's it. I'm a Gator."

There was a change in Dalvin's high school situation, as well. The Rockets' head coach, Telly Lockette, accepted a job as a running backs coach with the University of South Florida. Roland Smith became Dalvin's new head coach.

Coach Smith expanded Dalvin's role, playing him at cornerback and safety on defense.

In 2013, Dalvin attended a USC football camp. There, he worked out with some of the best athletes from other high schools. Upon returning home, he was told by Coach Smith to take the day off from practice; he'd worked hard at the camp.

Dalvin refused. If his team was practicing, he would practice with them.

"It was a hot, humid day," Coach Smith recalled. "90-some degrees and guess who's leading [the way]: Dalvin Cook."

Dalvin was that kind of leader. He would continue to work hard and inspire his teammates throughout his senior year at Central High School.

At football camps, players perform drills to improve their skills.

4

SENIOR SEASON

The Central Rockets football team went 9–1 during the 2013 regular season. In the first round of the playoffs, they beat Boynton Beach, 55–37. A week later, they routed Dillard High, 59–14.

On November 30, the team met the undefeated Heritage Panthers. With six minutes left in the first quarter, Yearby was tackled hard at the Panthers' 27-yard line. He went down and stayed down. He had fractured the fibula in his left leg. His game—and his season—were over.

Two plays later, Dalvin zipped into the end zone for Central's first score. The avalanche began. The Rockets dominated, gaining more than 500 yards in total offense. They won handily, 54–3. Dalvin contributed 244 yards and three touchdowns, including a 72-yard run.

On December 7, Central battled Daytona Beach Mainland. Dalvin warmed up in his familiar #4 jersey. But after warmups, he slipped back into the locker. He returned to the field wearing the Rockets' #3 jersey: Yearby's jersey.

Dalvin rushed for 73 yards in a 28–15 win. The victory put Central in the championship game for the fourth year in a row. It marked the first time any Miami-Dade team had played in four consecutive championships.

Dalvin sat on the bench with a towel on his head. There was just one more game to go. Then what? He had committed to play for the University of Florida, but was that the right fit? He was no longer certain.

Dalvin knew that he needed to follow his friend Davonta Freeman's advice: Do what his heart told him to do. But there was still a championship to win. He'd make his final decision after that.

Dalvin wore his #4 jersey against the 14–1 Armwood Hawks. He began the scoring a few minutes into the game. He eluded three defenders on his way to a 37-yard touchdown run.

A second Rockets' touchdown gave them a 14–0 lead at the end of the first quarter. The teams traded touchdowns in the second, and Central led, 21–7, at halftime.

The Rockets started the third quarter with the ball on their 15-yard line. A holding call wiped out Dalvin's first rush of nine yards. Three plays later, he picked up 23 yards for a first down. A 52-yard deep pass put Central at Armwood's six-yard line. There, Dalvin took it in for another touchdown.

The Rockets scored again, this time on a 43-yard return of an interception. Central was in complete control, 35–7.

Dalvin already had two touchdowns, but he wasn't finished. The first play of the fourth quarter saw him outrace the defense for an 80-yard score. When he reached the goal line, he flipped into the end zone. The showboating earned his team a 15-yard penalty for unsportsmanlike conduct.

Dalvin added a five-yard touchdown run after a blocked punt, and that capped the scoring at 52–7. The Central Rockets were once again champions. It was their third championship in four years.

The Hawks finished the game with 164 total yards. Dalvin contributed 223 of Central's 311 total yards, to go with his four touchdowns.

In his senior season, Dalvin posted 1,940 yards rushing on 177 carries, averaging 11.0 yards per carry—the best in the nation. He scored 34 touchdowns, and he also intercepted three passes on defense.

Dalvin was named Mr. Florida Football by the Florida Dairy Farmers Association. The honor was voted on by a panel of media representatives and high school coaches.

He was named to *USA Today's* All-USA Football Team, 247 Sports Second Team All-American, and All-State Class 6A first-team.

Dalvin finished his prep career with 4,267 rushing yards and 64 touchdowns. Between him and Yearby, the duo posted nearly 10,000 yards rushing in just three years.

Following his senior season, Dalvin was invited to play in the 2014 Under Armour All-America Game, held at Tropicana Field in Saint Petersburg, Florida. Dalvin rushed for 78 yards and a score on just eight carries, but his team lost the exhibition game, 31–21.

He also participated in "The Opening," an all-star football camp held on the Nike Campus in Oregon. The invite-only event allowed players to receive coaching from experienced trainers and to develop positive relationships with other high school players.

5
COLLEGE CHOICES

Dalvin had little time to celebrate his stellar senior year before the question began circulating again: Where would he go to college? Despite saying that he would be a Gator, he entertained coach Mack Brown from Texas and coach Jimbo Fisher from Florida State. He told the media that he wasn't ready to reveal his choice.

Davonta Freeman provided inspiration that seemed to tip the balance in Dalvin's decision. When Dalvin visited Florida State in Tallahassee, Freeman was his host. Freeman would be declaring for the NFL draft, leaving a starting spot wide open for Dalvin.

"Everything was just set up for me to go be successful," Dalvin later said. "I just had to go do it. [Freeman] created the blueprint for me."

On December 31, Dalvin committed to play for the Florida State University (FSU) Seminoles.

However, Dalvin's college football career was nearly derailed before it started. Reportedly, he tripped and suffered a labrum (cartilage) tear in his shoulder. He had surgery on March 8, 2014, and missed all of spring practice.

He began training with the second-team offense in the fall but soon caught the attention of Seminoles quarterback Jameis Winston. Dalvin constantly burned the starting defense. Winston asked to have Dalvin moved to the starting squad and said that he thought Dalvin would be the best running back in the country.

Coach Fisher noticed too. He was impressed by Dalvin's work ethic, as well as his talent. Dalvin would get his chance to compete for playing time.

Dalvin missed the opening game, a 37–31 victory over Oklahoma State University. But he made a strong impression in the team's second game, on September 6.

Against the Citadel Bulldogs, Dalvin led his team in rushing with 67 yards. He scored his first college touchdown early in the second quarter. FSU won, 37–12.

Dalvin continued to play a contributing role in the weeks that followed. Through his first five games, Dalvin gained 128 yards rushing. More importantly, his team won all five games.

The freshman truly got his chance to shine on October 11 against the Syracuse Orange. He rushed 23 times for 122 yards, and he scored FSU's final touchdown in a 38–20 win.

The Seminoles continued their winning ways, and Dalvin continued to take advantage of his opportunities. Against the Louisville Cardinals, Dalvin gained 110 yards on the ground and scored twice: in the third quarter on a 40-yard run and in the fourth from 38 yards out. The Seminoles improved their record to 8–0 with a 42–31 victory.

With a perfect record this late in the season, FSU was sure to qualify for one of the top post-season bowl games. The big question was "which one?" FSU was hoping for the Rose Bowl.

On November 15, the team traveled to Sun Life Stadium—just 10 minutes from Dalvin's home—

for a showdown with the Miami Hurricanes and Joseph Yearby.

It was time to settle the debate: Who was the better running back? Dalvin intended to come out on top.

Miami dominated at the start. Early in the second quarter, they held a 16–0 lead. FSU got their first score when Dalvin busted through the line and raced 44 yards to the end zone.

By the third quarter, the Hurricanes held a 23–10 lead. The Seminoles put a touchdown on the board late in the quarter.

In the fourth, the teams went back and forth, adding field goals to the score. FSU inched closer, but Miami held a 26–23 advantage with just over seven minutes to go.

The Seminoles took over at their own 38-yard line. Dalvin picked up 14 yards on a pass play then followed up with a 15-yard run, helping his team get within field goal range.

Dalvin and the Seminoles lined up on the Hurricanes' 26-yard line. Dalvin took the handoff and weaved around Hurricane defenders. He

Dalvin led his team with 67 yards rushing in his first college game.

eluded three tackles on his way to the goal line. Touchdown!

He threw his hands into the air and made a 3-0-5 with his fingers, which stood for the local area code—a symbol of Miami pride. By coincidence, the time remaining on the game clock was 3:05.

There was plenty of time for Miami's explosive offense to take back the lead, but the Seminoles intercepted a pass, sealing their victory. Florida State had notched their 10th win of the season.

To go with his two touchdowns, Dalvin totaled 92 rushing yards and 18 receiving yards. Yearby gained 34 yards on 10 attempts.

6

ROSE BOWL

With two games left in the regular season, the Seminoles were ranked as the best college football team in the nation.

FSU defeated Boston College, 20–17. Then they finished their perfect regular season with a 24–19 victory against the Florida Gators. Dalvin posted 144 yards rushing on 24 carries.

A record of 12–0 was more than enough to put the Seminoles in the Atlantic Coast Conference Championship on December 6. Their opponent was the Georgia Tech Yellow Jackets.

Early in the second quarter, Dalvin scored from one yard out. FSU scored twice more in the second quarter and led, 28–21, at halftime.

The Yellow Jackets tied the game in the third. But the Seminoles added three field goals, extending their lead to 37–28 in the fourth quarter.

Georgia Tech connected on a 25-yard touchdown pass with 1:47 left in the game. But the Yellow Jackets wouldn't get another chance to score. Dalvin and his team were victorious, 37–35.

Dalvin rose to the occasion, playing his best game of the season. He rushed for 177 yards and caught five passes for 43 yards. He was named the game's most valuable player.

A day later, it was announced that FSU would return to the Rose Bowl—a game they had won the prior year.

Dalvin had played in big games before—but nothing like this. The attention was intense. The winning team would move on to the College Football Playoff National Championship. The losing team would go home, their season over.

The Seminoles traveled to Pasadena, California, to meet the 12–1 Oregon Ducks on January 1, 2015. Despite being undefeated, FSU was the underdog. Oregon was expected to win by a very wide margin.

Those expectations were met.

The Seminoles stayed close in the first half, with 92 yards from Dalvin. At halftime, the Ducks led, 18–13.

In the third quarter, Dalvin fumbled twice, and Oregon turned those mistakes into two quick touchdowns.

More FSU mistakes led to more scores. Five minutes into the fourth quarter, the Ducks led, 59–20. Neither team scored in the game's final 10 minutes. The Oregon Ducks moved on to the national championship.

Dalvin finished his freshman season with 1,008 yards rushing and 203 yards receiving. He scored eight rushing touchdowns.

7

LEGAL TROUBLE

All-star quarterback Jameis Winston left the Seminoles after the season. He declared for the NFL draft and was selected by the Tampa Bay Buccaneers. With his departure, FSU intended to rely heavily on Dalvin for the 2015 season.

However, in July, Dalvin found himself in a troubling situation.

A woman reportedly got into a tense argument with some of Dalvin's teammates. She claimed that she pushed one of the players away from her and that Dalvin responded by hitting her.

Dalvin denied the accusation. Three teammates who were with him also said that he did not strike the woman. Still, he was charged with a misdemeanor crime of battery.

Coach Fisher took the matter very seriously. He suspended Dalvin from the team.

As the criminal investigation gained steam, Dalvin's past run-ins with the law—from when he was 13 and 14 years old—were reported. It also came to light that Dalvin had reportedly been involved in three other incidents during his freshman year.

In June 2014, he had been charged with criminal mischief. Dalvin (along with some other players) had allegedly caused property damage with a BB gun. He did not go to trial for the crime. Instead, he was given pre-trial intervention (PTI), a process that involved forms of discipline such as community service.

In July 2014, Dalvin seemed to be in the wrong place at the wrong time. He was in the company of two men who reportedly threatened a neighbor with a gun. Tallahassee police said that Dalvin was not a suspect, and Dalvin was never charged with a crime.

That same month, Dalvin had been cited for a form of animal cruelty. Three pit bull puppies were chained with heavy chains and were not provided proper shelter, according to the citation.

chains were too heavy for the puppies to move. punishment, Dalvin was fined $550.

In a Fox Sports article, writer Kelvin Hunt tried to defend Dalvin. "Where I grew up," Hunt wrote, "it was not uncommon for young teenagers to have a litter of puppies in this manner. I honestly think Cook did not view this as animal cruelty but was the norm in the environment where he grew up." Hunt added that this did not excuse the behavior.

Dalvin was a young man who had made a series of mistakes. It was time to grow up, time to make a change in his life.

Despite the suspension from the team, Dalvin knew that Coach Fisher supported him. The young running back vowed to do better and refocused himself on football.

During his time away from the team, Dalvin worked out, lifted weights, and trained to improve his speed. His brother DeAndre Burnett, who played basketball at the University of Mississippi, spent a week with Dalvin. The two of them practiced together, both on the football field and the basketball court.

Dalvin practiced running routes and catching passes. He spent time studying the playbook. When he was able to return to the team, Dalvin would be ready.

On August 25, 2015, Dalvin was put on trial for the charge of assault. The trial lasted 10 hours and was heard by a six-person jury.

After hearing both sides of the story, members of the jury quickly returned a verdict of not guilty.

The legal battle had ended. Dalvin was able to rejoin the football team.

8
BACK IN THE BACKFIELD

Dalvin came back even stronger and more determined. He adapted a more physical style of play. He was still fast enough to outrun his opponents, but now he could break tackles too.

Lockette, Dalvin's former high school coach, said he was just beginning to peak. "He is seeing things clearer in terms of seeing holes and reading defenders," Lockette said in *USA Today*.

In his first game, on September 5, Dalvin rushed for 156 yards and scored two touchdowns against Texas State. FSU won, 59–16.

A week later, Dalvin put his talents to use versus the South Florida Bulls. Late in the first quarter, Dalvin tore through the line of scrimmage, cut left, and sped away. A defensive back moved in for the tackle, but Dalvin hurdled him and kept running. He raced all the way to the end zone.

The Bulls kept the game close, evening the score at 7–7 before halftime. But less than two minutes into the third quarter, Dalvin outraced the defense for a 24-yard touchdown. Four minutes later, he took the ball from Florida State's 42-yard line and sped to South Florida's 15 before he was knocked out of bounds. The run set up a field goal for the Seminoles.

Dalvin scored the final touchdown of the game with 1:55 left, zipping 37 yards to the end zone. FSU won, 34–14.

Dalvin finished with a jaw-dropping 266 yards rushing on 30 carries to go with his three touchdowns.

After defeating Boston College, the Seminoles traveled to Wake Forest on October 3. On their second possession, the FSU offense took over at their own six-yard line. Dalvin got his first rushing attempt of the game—and he bolted 94 yards for a score.

A few minutes later, Dalvin caught a short pass out of the backfield. He turned upfield and gained a first down, but he reached for his left leg

In 2015, Dalvin rushed for more than 200 yards in a game—twice.

and hobbled out of bounds. He had injured his hamstring on the play, and he would not return for the rest of the 24–16 FSU win.

The injury was not severe. After a week of rehabilitation, Dalvin was able to play on October 10 against the Miami Hurricanes.

Dalvin had become a college phenomenon, garnering national attention. The media was now aware of his friendly rivalry with Joseph Yearby.

They were two of the best backs in the Atlantic Coast Conference (ACC), but Yearby was trailing Dalvin in yardage (570 to 424) and yards per carry (8.6 to 7.3). Both men were ready to put on a show.

As the game started, Dalvin began his bid to resolve talk of his injury. Three minutes into the first quarter, he took the football and dashed 72 yards for a touchdown. On the next series, Dalvin caught a short pass in the middle of the field and weaved his way to another score.

Early in the second quarter, Dalvin took a handoff and pounded out 35 yards—before pulling up and reaching for the same leg he had injured the week before.

He hobbled to the sideline, climbed on the trainer's table, and stretched the leg. But he didn't stay there long. On the next series, he returned to the game and tore off a 17-yard run.

Miami was a solid team, and they weren't going to let Dalvin steal the show. They kept the score within reach, and they took the lead early in the fourth quarter, 24–23.

Once again, Dalvin proved his worth. He scored, this time on a 23-yard run. Despite a failed two-point conversion, the touchdown was enough. FSU held on to win, 29–24, for their fifth straight victory of the season.

Dalvin posted 222 rushing yards, 47 receiving yards, and three touchdowns. He became the first player to gain at least 200 yards rushing twice in one season since 1981.

Yearby was held to 33 yards rushing, 15 yards receiving, and a touchdown.

9
TOUGH LOSSES

The Seminoles carried their winning ways into the next week, a home game against the Louisville Cardinals. Dalvin gained 163 yards rushing and scored two touchdowns in a 41–21 victory.

Up next was an easy game against the 2–5 Georgia Tech Yellow Jackets. However, no one told Georgia Tech they were supposed to lose. At the end of the game, the Yellow Jackets blocked FSU's game-winning field goal attempt and returned it 78 yards for the game-winning touchdown. FSU fell, 22–16.

Afterward, Dalvin told his coaches that he had injured his ankle. The Seminoles could not risk making the injury worse. Dalvin sat out for his team's 45–21 victory over Syracuse. They would need him fresh and rested against the undefeated Clemson Tigers.

Dalvin seemed to set the tone on the very first offensive play. After taking a handoff in the backfield, he darted through the front line and sped 75 yards for a touchdown. It was a thrilling start to a day in which Dalvin ran for 194 yards. It would be the only touchdown FSU scored. They fell to 7–2 on the season with a 23–13 loss.

A week later, the Seminoles returned to their winning ways against North Carolina State. Dalvin rushed for 138 yards and scored two touchdowns as his team won, 34–17. In the game, Dalvin set a new school record for most yards rushing in a season. The previous mark had been set in 1995 by Warrick Dunn (1,242 yards).

The Seminoles also won their final two games of the regular season. Dalvin gained 289 yards in the two games and scored four more touchdowns.

With a record of 10–2, the team was invited to play against the 12–1 Houston Cougars in the Chick-fil-A Peach Bowl.

Held on New Year's Eve, the game aired nationally on ESPN. The Seminoles were seven-point favorites, but many experts believed it would be decided by whichever superstar played better: Dalvin or Houston quarterback Greg Ward, Jr.

Both teams knew which player they had to stop. Houston did a better job of it. Their defense held Dalvin to 33 yards rushing, and the Cougars won the game, 38–24.

Still, it was a banner year for Dalvin. He played in 12 games and, despite injuries, gained 1,691 rushing yards (1,935 all-purpose yards), and scored 20 touchdowns. He positioned himself as one of the best players in college football.

10
SLOW START

The span between football seasons was less chaotic than the previous year, but there were challenges. On March 31, 2016, during spring practice, Dalvin again injured his shoulder. He again underwent surgery for a labrum tear. He was not able to play in the team's spring game, but he was ready by fall.

The new season got off to a shaky start. The team's starting quarterback suffered a broken foot, and the backup quarterback was suspended. So the Seminoles began the season with their third-string quarterback under center.

When the University of Mississippi Rebels rolled into town for the first game, they kept FSU contained. The Seminoles went into the locker room, trailing 28–13.

Dalvin's team opened the third quarter with a field goal and a quick turnover. That led to an FSU touchdown.

FSU scored again after a Rebels' fumble. The Seminoles took the lead, 29–28, and never looked back. They won the game, 45–34. Dalvin finished with 91 yards rushing and 101 yards receiving.

FSU also won their second game, but a week later, the Louisville Cardinals pummeled them by a score of 63–20.

On September 24, FSU walked onto South Florida's football field with something to prove. The Bulls were undefeated, but Dalvin and his team had plans to change that.

Just seconds into the game, South Florida connected on an 84-yard touchdown pass. Not to be outdone, the Seminoles handed the ball to Dalvin on the next offensive play. He took it 75 yards for a score. After just 28 seconds, the scoreboard stood at 7–7.

The Bulls answered with a rushing touchdown. Two minutes later, Dalvin scored his second touchdown, on a 13-yard scamper.

Florida State's cheerleaders get the crowd excited before football games.

The Seminoles added two more touchdowns in the first quarter and another 10 points in the second. They went into halftime ahead, 38–14.

Throughout the second half, FSU maintained a comfortable lead. They won the game, 55–35.

Dalvin amassed 267 yards rushing and 62 yards receiving to go with his two early touchdowns.

The North Carolina Tar Heels came to town the next week. The Seminoles struggled from the opening whistle. The offense couldn't seem to get going and the defense was inconsistent. The Tar Heels scored three touchdowns before Dalvin finally put FSU on the board. Late in the second quarter, He scored on a nine-yard touchdown run.

He added touchdown runs of one and three yards in the fourth quarter, helping his team rally to a 28–28 tie.

North Carolina put together an impressive drive that resulted in a touchdown with 2:31 on the clock. The extra point attempt was blocked.

The Seminoles had one last chance, and they turned to Dalvin. He caught a 41-yard pass that put FSU on North Carolina's 18-yard line. The thrilling play led to a touchdown run by FSU quarterback Deondre Francois.

After a successful extra point, the Seminoles held their first lead of the game, 35–34, with 23 seconds to go.

However, on North Carolina's next possession, a pass interference penalty put the ball on FSU's 37-yard line. On the final play of the game, the Tar Heels attempted a 54-yard field goal. The kick went up and squeaked just inside the right upright.

The Seminoles dropped their second game of the season in a 37–35 heartbreaker. Dalvin finished the day with 140 yards rushing, 106 yards receiving, and three touchdowns.

11
SCORING TOUCHDOWNS

The Seminoles were 3–2 on the season and 0–2 in their conference. Fans and media wondered if it was already a lost year.

FSU's schedule didn't get any easier. They met their old rivals, the 4–0 Miami Hurricanes. The Hurricanes dominated the first half and took a 13–3 advantage into halftime.

Midway through the third quarter, Dalvin scored on a 59-yard reception. Five minutes later, the Seminoles scored again, giving them a 17–13 lead. They extended their advantage in the fourth quarter with a field goal.

Miami waited until their final possession of the game to respond. They found the end zone with 1:38 left in regulation. However, the extra-point attempt failed. FSU escaped with a narrow 20–19 victory.

Dalvin tallied 27 rushes for 150 yards to go with his lone reception, a 59-yard touchdown.

The Seminoles won again a week later, 17–6, versus Wake Forest. Dalvin ran for 115 yards.

The Clemson Tigers came to Tallahassee on October 29. The Tigers were 8–0 in their quest for a national championship. They started fast, scoring twice in the first quarter to take a 14–0 lead.

The Seminoles came back midway through the second on a four-yard touchdown run by Dalvin. Clemson put up a field goal late in the half, but FSU added a touchdown before halftime, cutting Clemson's lead to 17–14.

Dalvin broke off a 43-yard touchdown run in the third quarter. He topped that a few minutes later with a 70-yard touchdown run, giving his team a 28–20 advantage.

Clemson scored a touchdown early in the fourth and added a field goal to regain the lead. The Seminoles answered with an eight-yard touchdown run by Dalvin. They had the lead again, 34–29, with three minutes left to play. But the Tigers found the end zone once more. FSU fell, 37–34.

Dalvin had a fantastic game, scoring four of the Seminoles' five touchdowns. He gained 169 yards on the ground.

The following week, the Seminoles defeated North Carolina State, 24-20. Then they blew out the Boston College Eagles, 45–7.

Dalvin's 108 yards rushing versus the Eagles put him in an elite class. He became the first Seminole to rush for more than 100 yards against Boston College since 1980.

On top of that, Dalvin only needed 19 more yards to reach 3,960 career rushing yards, which would set a new record at FSU.

He did it the next week against Syracuse. It wasn't on his first play, which was an incomplete pass. It wasn't on his second play, a five-yard run. The record-breaker came midway through the first quarter—when Dalvin broke off a 41-yard run to the Orange's 14-yard line. The play set up a touchdown for FSU.

The Seminoles handled the Orange, winning 45–14, and improved their record to 8–3. On the day, Dalvin totaled 225 yards on the ground. He crossed the goal line four times. Not only did he break FSU's rushing record, but he also became the sixth back in ACC history to gain more than 4,000 career yards. He was the first to accomplish this feat in only three seasons.

The Seminoles' final game of the regular season was at home against the Florida Gators. Dalvin started the scoring with a touchdown in the first quarter, and the Seminoles never lost the lead. They held the Gators to 13 points, while scoring 31 of their own. Dalvin netted 153 yards rushing.

More importantly, the Seminoles had salvaged their season. With a record of 9–3, they were sure to get invited to a top-notch bowl game.

12
ORANGE BOWL

The talk surrounding Florida State wasn't just about which bowl game they'd play in. Dalvin was going to be eligible for the upcoming National Football League (NFL) Draft. Would he choose to return to college for one more year? Or would he enter the draft and begin his professional career? As one of the most talented players in college, he would be selected by one of the 32 teams. In fact, he was projected to be a first-round draft pick.

Dalvin remained silent about his decision, choosing only to talk about Tallahassee and FSU. "I love everything we have going on here," Dalvin said. "It's really like my second home . . . I love it."

FSU got its answer to the other question on December 4. The NCAA announced that the Seminoles would meet the Michigan Wolverines in the Capital One Orange Bowl. Michigan had finished 10–2 in the regular season and was ranked sixth in the nation. FSU was ranked 11th.

The Orange Bowl was played on December 30 at Hard Rock Stadium in Miami Gardens, Florida. That was just 15 miles north of Dalvin's hometown.

With friends and family in the crowd, Dalvin hoped to put on a show.

FSU began the game on offense and put together a nice drive. A penalty for pass interference placed the ball on Michigan's two-yard line. Dalvin punched it in from there. The Seminoles were up, 7–0, three minutes into the game.

A few plays later, an FSU fumble set Michigan up with a first down at the one-yard line. But the Seminoles' defense knocked the Wolverines back and forced them to settle for a field goal.

Florida State began their next drive with a long pass to Dalvin. The connection went for 45 yards to Michigan's 30-yard line. The play led to a field goal for the Seminoles.

FSU struck again a few minutes later. Wide receiver Nyqwan Murray waltzed into the end zone courtesy of a 92-yard connection from quarterback

Deondre Francois. It was a new record for the longest touchdown pass in Orange Bowl history. The first quarter ended with FSU leading, 17–3.

Each team added a field goal in the second quarter, and the Seminoles held a 20–6 lead at halftime.

The Wolverines stormed back in the third with nine straight points. And by the time the fourth quarter began, FSU had lost momentum. A holding penalty and a sack had the team out of sync.

Facing third down—with 22 yards to go for a first down—the Seminoles again turned to Dalvin. He took the handoff, stumbled near the 15-yard line, regained his balance, and raced down the left sideline for an incredible 71 yards.

Four plays later, a touchdown put the Seminoles ahead, 27–15.

There was no quit in the Wolverines. They responded with two touchdowns and a successful two-point conversion. Just like that, Michigan led for the first time in the game, 30–27.

With only 1:57 on the clock, the Seminoles were in need of a big play. They got it. Kickoff returner

Keith Gavin rumbled 66 yards before being brought down at Michigan's 34.

On first down, Dalvin caught a pass while crossing the middle of the field, toward the right sideline. He made a quick move to his left and rumbled forward for a 21-yard gain.

A few plays later, Francois zipped a pass to Murray in the end zone. A spectacular leaping catch over a defender gave FSU the lead again, 33–30, with 36 seconds on the clock.

The point-after attempt was blocked, ending an NCAA record of 302 straight extra points for FSU. To make matters worse, Michigan picked up the loose ball and returned it to their end zone for two points. Florida State was only up by a point.

But the Seminoles defense ended the game with an interception. FSU won the Orange Bowl in what might have been Dalvin's final college game.

Dalvin was named the bowl's MVP, an award that was richly deserved. He rushed 20 times for 145 yards, caught three passes for 62 yards, and scored a touchdown. All told, Dalvin netted 207 of FSU's 371 yards.

Dalvin scored 46 rushing touchdowns in three seasons with Florida State.

DOUGLAS

"Being in [the Orange Bowl] was a childhood dream," he said.

Like his team, Dalvin finished the year strong. Despite his slow start in 2013, he improved upon his record-breaking previous season. He posted 1,765 yards rushing and added 488 receiving yards, giving him an astounding total of 2,253 yards from scrimmage.

His career rushing yardage totaled 4,464. That ranked second on the list of all-time ACC rushers (just behind Ted Brown, who put up 4,602 yards for North Carolina State from 1975 to 1978).

Not only was Dalvin second all-time in rushing in the ACC, he ranked first all-time in yards from scrimmage with 5,399.

He was recognized as one of the best players in the nation when he was a unanimous selection to the College Football All-America Team. He was only the second Seminole running back to receive the honor.

13

RUMORS

The question on everyone's mind at FSU was whether Dalvin would return for his senior year. The media turned to Coach Fisher for answers.

"I don't know that," Fisher said. "But I know one thing. If we get him, we'll be the luckiest team in the world. Whoever drafts him will be the luckiest team in the world. Somebody is going to be happy."

Fisher went on to say that Dalvin would always be part of the Seminole family, and he wished his star player the best.

A day after the Orange Bowl, on December 31, Dalvin announced his decision during an Instagram live feed. He decided to enter the 2017 NFL Draft.

NBC Sports projected that Dalvin would get drafted in the first round.

Lance Zierlein of NFL.com said that Dalvin was a "home run hitter with a resume featuring monster games against his most highly regarded opponents." Zierlein speculated that Dalvin could be an NFL "rookie of the year candidate right away." However, he added a word of caution: Dalvin's value "could be diminished by injuries, character, and issues in pass protection."

On March 3, 2017, Dalvin attended the NFL Draft Combine. The event allowed top college players to showcase their football skills in a series of tests. NFL coaches and scouts analyzed the players to determine whether or not they wanted to draft each player—and in which round.

Dalvin's performance cast more doubt on his first-round chances. He did not do as well as NFL teams had hoped.

Still, Dalvin had plenty of in-game highlights that teams could study. Based on that, he remained a first-round prospect. After all, the combine simply measured speed, strength and leaping ability. It could not measure his desire to win, thirst for competition, and game-day success.

On March 27, Dalvin got another chance to showcase his abilities. Florida State held its pro day, at which coaches and scouts could take a look at the Seminoles' NFL hopefuls.

Dalvin performed much better in the familiar surroundings of FSU. The Philadelphia Eagles even stayed an extra day to privately work out Dalvin. The Eagles held the 14th pick in the draft, and many believed that Dalvin would be their choice.

However, just days before the draft, reports surfaced that Dalvin was showing up late to his workouts—or not showing up at all. It was also said that he was spending time with people of questionable character, which might lead to trouble.

Concerned NFL teams began calling Dalvin's trainer, Tony Villani.

Robert Klemko of *Sports Illustrated* spoke with Villani about the rumors.

Villani said, "I told [the NFL teams], 'You know me. You know I'm not going to lie to you. You've got it wrong.'"

Klemko was able to find the alleged source of the rumors. It was a "runner," a person who carried messages back and forth between college players and NFL agents. Villani had reportedly dealt with the runner before and had problems with the person due to an overdue training bill.

Dalvin said that he did not know the runner, so it was a mystery why Dalvin was targeted.

Despite Villani's confirmation that the rumors were false, the news came at a bad time. Dalvin could only wait and see how they would affect his draft position.

14

A NEW TEAM

The first round of the 2017 NFL Draft was held on April 27 in Philadelphia, Pennsylvania. Dalvin spent the evening at home, hosting a draft party with his family and friends.

"They all helped me get to where I'm at today," he said in an interview. He felt it was important to spend the biggest moments of his life with them.

As it turned out, Dalvin's moment had to wait another day. His name was not called in the first round. In fact, not a single Seminole was chosen.

The first round was dominated by defensive choices, but a couple of running backs went off the board. Leonard Fournette was chosen fourth by the Jacksonville Jaguars, and Christian McCaffrey went eighth to the Carolina Panthers. The fact that Dalvin was not drafted seemed to again call into question his character, fueled by ugly rumors.

Dalvin and his family would see what Day 2 of the draft brought. One team was very interested in the young running back. Dalvin spent 45 minutes talking to Rick Spielman, general manager of the Minnesota Vikings.

Minnesota was in need of a new running back. A few days earlier, the team had released former All-Pro—and perhaps the best running back in team history—Adrian Peterson.

Peterson's departure left a big hole to fill. In 10 years with the Vikings, Peterson had amassed 11,747 rushing yards, scored 97 touchdowns, and averaged a spectacular 4.9 yards per carry. He set several franchise records, including the Vikings' rookie rushing record.

The second round got underway, and the Green Bay Packers traded into the first pick. They were light on running backs too; perhaps Dalvin was their choice. The Packers selected a defensive back instead.

Picks 34, 35, 36, and 37 went by. Dalvin waited. Picks 38, 39, and 40 passed, and still Dalvin was without a team.

"He was sticking out like a sore thumb on top of our [list of best players]," said Spielman.

Unfortunately for the Vikings, there will still eight picks to go before they would get their turn. It seemed unlikely that Dalvin would remain available until them. Someone was going to get him—and soon. The Vikings needed to make a trade if they hoped to draft him.

The Cincinnati Bengals held the 41st pick, and the Vikings offered them the 48th pick plus a fourth-round pick in order to move up.

The Bengals accepted, and Dalvin Cook's wait finally ended. He was drafted by the Vikings with the ninth pick in the second round.

Big changes were happening in Dalvin's life—and not just on the football field. Not long after he was drafted, his girlfriend, Jacquilla Morris, gave birth to a baby boy. Dalvin was a new father.

In the months that followed, Dalvin spent countless hours preparing for his first NFL season. He worked hard to get stronger and faster. He learned the Vikings' playbook. He got to know his new coaches and teammates.

Dalvin was drafted by the Minnesota Vikings.

On July 23, Dalvin attended his first professional training camp at Minnesota State University in Mankato. He made an immediate impression on his coaches.

"This guy is different than other guys," head coach Mike Zimmer said in a *Sports Illustrated* interview. "The first thing the veteran players I've talked to about him say is, 'This guy gets it.'"

The Vikings played four preseason (practice) games during the month of August. Dalvin saw limited action in three of them. He looked steady but not spectacular. All told, he rushed 17 teams for 70 yards and caught six passes for 35 yards.

Expectations were high. Could Dalvin fill the void left by Peterson? Only time would tell.

15
SHORT SEASON

Despite his limited playing time during the 2017 preseason, Dalvin impressed the Vikings. The rookie was named a starter on September 5. He won the spot over Latavius Murray, whom the Vikings had signed during the offseason.

Murray was a Pro Bowl running back who had spent four seasons with the Oakland Raiders, and he came to Minnesota expecting to start. He had no hard feelings, though. He said that Dalvin had earned the spot.

The Vikings opened the regular season in a nationally televised Monday night game against the New Orleans Saints. The game held special meaning because Adrian Peterson would be playing his first NFL game against the Vikings.

For the former Viking, it was a frustrating night. He rushed just six times for 18 yards. Meanwhile,

Dalvin stayed busy, carrying the football 22 times in the game. A 33-yard run late in the contest set a new team record for the most yards rushing in a rookie debut. Dalvin finished the night with 127 yards on the ground, and the Vikings won, 29–19.

The following week, the Vikings traveled to Pittsburgh with an uncertain future. Starting quarterback Sam Bradford had injured his knee against the Saints. Backup Case Keenum was announced as the starter.

It was hard for the Vikings to get anything going against the Steelers. Dalvin led the Vikings with 64 yards rushing, but Minnesota fell, 26–9.

A week later, Dalvin found the end zone for his first professional score, at home against the Tampa Bay Buccaneers. The Vikings went to Dalvin on six of seven plays during their opening drive, including a 16-yard pass that took the Vikings to Tampa Bay's one-yard line. Two plays later, Dalvin dove over the middle of the goal line for the score.

"It was a good feeling knowing I got in," Dalvin told the *Pioneer Press*. "Coming out and scoring a touchdown in front of the home crowd was good."

Dalvin rushed for 97 yards in a 34–17 rout of the Buccaneers. He also caught five passes for 72 yards. In the process, he broke another record formerly held by Peterson: the three-game rookie rushing record. Dalvin's three-game total was 288 yards, beating Peterson's mark of 271 set in 2007.

For a team that had only managed 1,205 yards rushing the previous year, Dalvin offered the Vikings new hope for their ground game. He was well on his way to an unforgettable rookie season.

His work ethic was noticed by coaches and teammates. Vikings safety Harrison Smith said, "He's a tremendous back. We are lucky to have him. For a rookie, he is extremely composed. He just knows how to do the right things."

The Detroit Lions rolled into Minneapolis the following week to take on the rival Vikings. The game was controlled by each team's defense. Dalvin found the end zone in the second quarter, and the Vikings ended the half leading, 7–3.

A Vikings turnover early in the third quarter led to a Detroit field goal that cut the lead to 7–6. Dalvin got the football on Minnesota's next offensive play. He raced up the middle for 10 yards then tried to cut to his right to avoid a tackle. His left foot remained planted too long, his knee bent sideways, and Dalvin dropped to the ground. The ball came free, and Detroit recovered the fumble.

For Dalvin, it would be his final appearance in the game. His knee was injured, and it was potentially serious.

The Lions took advantage of the turnover. They added a touchdown and a two-point conversion. It gave them the lead—and eventually the win—with a final score of 14–7.

Dalvin missed almost an entire half of play, but he was still the NFL's third leading rusher. His injury was concerning.

The next day, Vikings coach Mike Zimmer announced that Dalvin had torn his anterior cruciate ligament (ACL). It was a relatively common sports injury, but it would require surgery to repair.

Dalvin's rookie season was over.

16
INJURY-PLAGUED

Dalvin went in for surgery on October 9. The procedure was deemed a success, and Dalvin reached out to his fans on Twitter. He thanked them for their prayers and thoughts and said that he was on the "road to recovery."

By November 16, Dalvin had left the crutches behind and had resumed weight training. There was a long way to go before he could rejoin his teammates on the field, but Dalvin was intent to be at full health for training camp in 2018.

By late April, he was able to participate with the team in strength and conditioning work.

"I attacked this thing every day," Dalvin said. "I did what I needed to do to get to this point."

Less than two months later, Dalvin was cleared to participate in full-team drills. Coach Zimmer and the Vikings were cautious with him at first, limiting his workload during practice. A player might be a little nervous after an injury like Dalvin's. The Vikings worked to rebuild the young back's confidence.

By the end of July, Dalvin felt comfortable with where he was, and he was ready to get on the field again. He put on the pads for full-contact practice in August. He was finally 100% back. There were no limits put on how hard he could practice.

Still, he did not play much during Minnesota's preseason. It was more important that he be ready and healthy for the season ahead. Dalvin took a couple of handoffs in the third preseason game, but he was otherwise kept off the field.

The regular season began on September 9, 2018, at home against the San Francisco 49ers. The Vikings split rushing duties between Dalvin and Latavius Murray. Dalvin gained 40 yards on 16 carries, and he caught six passes for 55 yards in a 24–16 win.

The following week, the Vikings played Green Bay to a 29–29 overtime tie. Dalvin put together 38 yards on the ground and 52 yards receiving. But he suffered an injury during overtime when he was crunched on a tackle.

He later reported that he had gone down with cramps and that it wasn't anything serious. But he did not practice in the days that followed. It was revealed that he had suffered a hamstring injury and would miss the next game. Fans began to worry about Dalvin being prone to injuries. Dalvin promised he would only be out for one game.

Without him, the Vikings were humiliated at home, 27–6, by the underdog Buffalo Bills.

True to his word, Dalvin suited up and took the field against the Los Angeles Rams. He gained 20 yards rushing in the first half, but he was kept out of the second half. Minnesota lost one of the most exciting and entertaining games of the NFL season, 38–31.

Dalvin wasn't upset about getting benched. The Vikings were being careful with him. That was understandable. Dalvin said that it felt "really good" just to be out there.

It was apparent that Minnesota needed Dalvin back to full health as soon as possible. After four weeks, the Vikings were averaging only 63 yards rushing per game—second worst in the league.

They would have a hard time improving that total against the Philadelphia Eagles on October 7. The Eagles had the best run defense in the league.

"This thing is still healing up," Dalvin said about his injury. "I want to be 100 percent as bad as everybody else wants me to be 100 percent. But I'm just not there yet."

Dalvin was not on the field for the game against Philadelphia, but his team put together a solid performance. The Vikings won, 23–21.

He suited up the next week against the Arizona Cardinals. However, during pregame warmups, the training staff determined the he was not ready. The Vikings won behind 155 yards rushing from Murray and improved their record to 3–2–1.

Dalvin also missed Minnesota's 37–17 victory over the New York Jets and a 30–20 loss to the New Orleans Saints.

17

PLAYOFF CHASE

After missing five of the first eight games, Dalvin walked onto the field at U.S. Bank Stadium to face the Detroit Lions. He had just 10 rushing attempts, but he tallied 89 yards on the ground, including a career-long 70-yard explosion late in the second quarter. Dalvin also chipped in with 20 yards receiving in the Vikings' 24–9 win.

Dalvin was, in his own words, "hyped" for the game in Chicago. The Bears were 6–3 on the season, and the Vikings held a 5–3–1 record. If Minnesota won, they would move ahead of the Bears into first place in the National Football Conference (NFC) North division.

The Bears had only allowed one rushing touchdown in nine games, and their stout run defense held up against the Vikings.

Dalvin gained only 12 yards on the ground. The Vikings lost, 25–20.

The following week, Dalvin scored on a 26-yard touchdown reception against the Green Bay Packers. He otherwise gained just 29 yards on the ground to go with 47 through the air. It was enough to give his team the victory, 24–17.

He fared better the next week in New England, rushing nine times for 84 yards. However, the Patriots rolled over the Vikings, 24–10.

A similar story played out in a 21–7 loss to the Seattle Seahawks. Dalvin scored late in the fourth quarter on a six-yard pass reception. The Seahawks held him to 55 yards rushing.

The Vikings play their home games at U.S. Bank Stadium.

After the loss, the team's offensive coordinator, John DeFilippo, was fired. The Vikings replaced him by promoting their quarterbacks coach, Kevin Stefanski.

Despite the offensive struggles, the Vikings were still in the hunt for a playoff berth with a 6–6–1 record.

When the 7–6 Miami Dolphins came to town on December 16, Dalvin rumbled for 136 yards rushing and two touchdowns. The Vikings played arguably their best game of the season and won handily, 41–17.

The Vikings also rolled past the Detroit Lions, 27–9. On 16 attempts, Dalvin gained 73 yards rushing. He also chipped in with three catches for 35 yards.

At 8–6–1, the Vikings could clinch a playoff spot with a win over Chicago. The Bears had already clinched the division title.

Unfortunately for Minnesota, the visiting team cruised past the Vikings, 24–10. Dalvin was limited to 39 yards, and the Vikings were held to a season-low total of 164 yards. It was a disappointing end to a see-saw season.

In 2018, Dalvin played in 11 of 17 games. He rushed the ball 133 times for 615 yards, an average of 4.6 yards per carry. He also caught 40 passes for 305 yards. Dalvin scored two touchdowns rushing and two receiving.

It wasn't the season he'd hoped for. But he believed that 2019 would prove to be better.

18
PLAYER OF THE WEEK

Dalvin had missed a lot of games in his first two years, and it was easy to call him injury-prone. Still, it was important to remember that during his college career he had only missed three games due to injury.

Ahead of the 2019 season, he was ready to prove that he was not only reliable but also one of the best running backs in the NFL.

Dalvin received limited carries during the preseason: all of them in the third game, versus the Arizona Cardinals. Dalvin gained three yards with his first attempt. A four-yard-run was nullified by a penalty. On his final carry of the preseason, the running back showed his speed, balance, and vision on a handoff that he took 85 yards for a touchdown. It was the longest preseason run in Minnesota Vikings history.

On September 8, the Vikings faced the Atlanta Falcons in the first game of the regular season. For Dalvin, the day was extra special. After nearly a decade of following Devonta Freeman through high school, college, and into the NFL, Dalvin finally got to share the field with his friend, mentor, and inspiration.

Freeman had been voted to the Pro Bowl two times. It was an exhibition game at the end of every season that featured the best players in the league.

Like Dalvin, Freeman was coming off an injury. Both men were looking to get back to top form.

Dalvin fared better than his counterpart. In the Vikings' 28–12 win, Dalvin rushed 21 times for 111 yards and scored two touchdowns. Freeman totaled just 19 yards on eight carries.

After the game, the two running backs traded their jerseys. For all the success Dalvin had on the field, it seemed as if this moment was the highlight of his day.

The Green Bay Packers knew what they needed to do when the Vikings visited Lambeau Field in Week 2: shut down Dalvin.

The Packers offense seemed unstoppable in the first quarter. They posted 21 points. They wouldn't score again, but the Vikings spent the rest of the game playing catch-up. Minnesota had to rely on their passing attack. Quarterback Kirk Cousins completed less than half of his throws and threw two interceptions. Dalvin gained 154 yards rushing, including a 75-yard touchdown.

The Vikings lost, 21–16, but Dalvin was named the FedEx Ground Player of the Week. He also joined an elite group of Vikings greats, by gaining 311 all-purpose yards in the first two games of a season. The only players ever to gain more were Gene Washington in 1969 (324 yards) and Adrian Peterson in 2009 (314 yards).

When the Oakland Raiders came to U.S. Bank Stadium the next week, Dalvin ran for 110 yards and scored a touchdown. After Minnesota's 34–14 rout, Dalvin was the NFL's leading rusher. His 375 yards over three games set a franchise record. He was also the first running back in Vikings history to rush for more than 100 yards in each of the first three games of the season.

More importantly, the win was the 500th in franchise history. It was a big day for Dalvin and for the Vikings.

Next, the Vikings marched into Soldier Field intending to run Dalvin through the Chicago Bears defense. However, the Bears stifled Dalvin and the Vikings. They sacked Cousins six times and held Dalvin to 35 yards on the day. Dalvin scored the Vikings' only touchdown, a two-yard run, in the 16–6 loss.

Now 2–2 on the season—and 0–2 against NFC North opponents—the Vikings were frustrated. They had worked hard to establish a running game. But their passing game was suffering. They were second-worst in the league in passing yards.

"At some point," wide receiver Adam Thielen said, "you're not going to be able to run the ball for 180 yards, even with the best running back in the NFL. That's when you have to be able to throw the ball . . . . You have to be able to hit the deep balls."

Thielen got a chance to prove his point the next week when Minnesota took on the New York Giants. The Vikings played a more balanced game, and Minnesota won easily, 28–10. Thielen caught seven passes for 130 yards and scored two touchdowns. Dalvin contributed 132 yards rushing and 86 yards receiving.

Another balanced effort helped Minnesota defeat the Philadelphia Eagles at home in Week 6. Dalvin was held to 41 yards, but he scored a touchdown in an impressive 38–20 victory.

The star running back got back on track in a big way against the Detroit Lions. He rushed for 142 yards and scored two touchdowns.

Dalvin's stellar performance won him another FedEx Ground Player of the Week award. More importantly, the Vikings won their third straight game, 42–30.

The Vikings escaped a scrappy battle against the Washington Redskins. Dalvin gained 98 yards on the ground and scored the game's only touchdown. Minnesota earned a 19–9 victory.

With half the season over, the NFC North was up for grabs. Minnesota had a chance to claim the top spot and carry their success into the playoffs.

19
SHOULDER PAIN

Against the Kansas City Chiefs, Dalvin rushed for 71 yards but was kept out of the end zone. The Vikings lost a close contest, 26–23.

A week later, they played another tight game in Dallas. Dalvin rumbled into the end zone from two yards out, late in the third quarter. It put Minnesota ahead, 28–21, and the Vikings held on to win, 28–24.

Dalvin finished with 97 yards rushing. He was also the team's top receiver, catching seven passes for 86 yards. He led the NFL with 1,415 yards from scrimmage.

The performance garnered him the honor of NFC Offensive Player of the Week. He became only the second Vikings running back to receive that honor twice. Dalvin also became the first

Against Washington, Dalvin had 98 rushing yards, 73 receiving yards, and a touchdown.

VIKINGS

NFL player since 2006 to gain more than 1,400 yards from scrimmage and score 10 touchdowns.

He was having the season that he always knew he could. With six games left on the schedule, there was no telling what records he might break.

The underdog Denver Broncos, with a record of 2–6, visited Minnesota on November 17. Denver played an exceptional first half and led, 20–0.

In the second half, quarterback Kirk Cousins peppered the ball around the field. Minnesota put one score on the board and entered the fourth quarter trailing, 23–7.

Dalvin scored a touchdown from three yards out. Then Cousins added two touchdowns, as the Vikings came roaring from behind to steal the victory, 27–23.

The momentum didn't last. Minnesota lost to the Seattle Seahawks. In case that wasn't bad enough, Dalvin took a hard hit in the third quarter that sent him to the locker room. He returned to the sidelines, but he did not enter the game again.

Tom Pelissero of the NFL Network reported that Dalvin had suffered a shoulder injury. It had first occurred against the Broncos, and it had been aggravated against the Seahawks. No bones were broken, but the spot was tender and caused a great deal of pain when contacted.

"It's a weird injury that I've got," Dalvin said. "It's kind of like when I land in an awkward spot, it hurts."

It would be difficult for Minnesota to make the playoffs without their star running back. There was a lot of work to do, and Dalvin had to be ready.

"I'll be good to go," Dalvin told NFL.com about the upcoming game against the Detroit Lions.

He did play—and Minnesota went back to a more balanced attack. But Dalvin shared the running duties a little more than usual in their 20–7 win. He ran 18 times for 62 yards and a touchdown. Alexander Mattison chipped in with 14 rushes, and Mike Boone took the ball five times.

Dalvin downplayed the severity of his injury, but his production had decreased significantly. Before the injury, he had been averaging 99 yards rushing and 42 yards receiving per game. He also scored 10 touchdowns in 10 games. In the four games since, Dalvin averaged 36 yards rushing and 24 yards receiving. At least he still managed to score touchdowns in each contest.

When the Vikings met the San Diego Chargers in Week 15, Dalvin played against an old Florida State teammate and friend, safety Derwin James.

Early in the third quarter, with the Vikings leading 19–10, Dalvin was popped for a three-yard loss. The tackle irritated Dalvin's shoulder, and he was pulled out of the game. The Vikings won handily, 39–10. But the injury meant that Dalvin would not play for the rest of the regular season.

Two days after the game, the roster for the Pro Bowl was announced. Dalvin was named a starter for the NFC. He led all running backs with 431,748 fan votes. In fact, only three players in the entire league received more votes: Lamar Jackson, Russell Wilson, and Patrick Mahomes—all quarterbacks.

On December 21, the Vikings were aided by the San Francisco 49ers. The 49ers defeated the Los Angeles Rams in a Saturday night game. With the Rams' loss, the Vikings were assured a spot in the playoffs.

Without Dalvin in the lineup, Minnesota lost their last two games and ended the regular season at 10–6. Fortunately for the team, Dalvin would be back and ready for the postseason.

20

NEW ORLEANS

If the Vikings hoped to advance in the playoffs, they would have to defeat the New Orleans Saints. Two years earlier, the teams had met in the playoffs at U.S. Bank Stadium. That game ended with a game-winning miracle touchdown by Minnesota on the final play.

This time, the Vikings were on the Saints' home field. New Orleans was 13–3, and most experts expected them to win.

The Saints began the scoring with a field goal in the first quarter. The Vikings answered with one of their own. Saints running back Alvin Kamara scored the first touchdown of the game on a four-yard rush in the second. The Viking fought back with a field goal late in the half, then their star running back scored his first postseason touchdown from five yards out.

The third quarter was a defensive struggle, but another touchdown from Dalvin—a one-yard plunge—gave the Vikings a 20–10 lead.

The Saints did not yield. They battled back with 10 points in the fourth quarter, and the clock struck zero with the score tied, 20–20. The game would be decided in overtime.

The Vikings got the ball first, and they gave it to Dalvin. He rushed for 20 yards on three carries to get the offense moving.

New Orleans knew they had to stop him, so when Cousins handed the ball to him again, the defense was ready. Except Dalvin didn't have the ball. Cousins had faked a handoff to him and instead fired a deep pass that receiver Adam Thielen caught at the Saints' two-yard line.

Three plays later, Cousins threw a touchdown pass to tight end Kyle Rudolph. The game was over. The Vikings had shocked New Orleans and knocked them out of the playoffs.

Dalvin was instrumental in the 26–20 win. He gained 94 yards on the ground, 36 yards through the air, and scored two touchdowns.

Minnesota's next opponent would be the 13–3 San Francisco 49ers. In the week leading up to the game, Dalvin fielded questions about his injuries.

"What injury?" he asked a reporter. "I'm good. Everybody on the team's good."

The 49ers knew that to win they would need to shut down Dalvin. The Vikings had won six of the seven games in which Dalvin rushed for 90 yards or more. So it wasn't just a matter of keeping Dalvin out of the end zone. It was keeping Dalvin from gaining yards.

That's exactly what San Francisco did.

The 49ers swarmed the Vikings' offensive line. They sacked Cousins six times and held Dalvin to 18 yards rushing. They dominated the game on both sides of the ball. The 49ers handed Minnesota a 27–10 loss and ended the Vikings' season.

Still, Dalvin and a few of his teammates had one more game to play.

On January 26, 2020, Dalvin attended his first Pro Bowl. Fellow Vikings Kirk Cousins and C.J. Ham joined him on offense. Danielle Hunter, Xavier Rhodes, Eric Kendricks, Everson Griffen,

Dalvin played in the 2020 Pro Bowl with some of the NFL's biggest stars.

and Harrison Smith helped shore up the NFC's defense.

The game was played in Orlando, Florida, a three-hour drive from where Dalvin grew up. During the week, Dalvin spent time with friends and family. He enjoyed being back in his home state and was honored to be part of the Pro Bowl.

He was used sparingly during the contest, which was mostly a passing attack. He carried the ball three times for 17 yards. Cousins, on the other hand, threw for 181 yards and two touchdowns, despite sharing quarterback duties with two other players. Their NFC team fell short in an offensive shootout, 38–33.

But for Dalvin, being a part of the all-star game was a fitting reward for a spectacular year—and for all the years of hard work, practice, and determination.

SPORTS BOOKS FOR THE WHOLE FAMILY TO ENJOY

Adam Thielen
Football biography
$12.95 retail

James Conner
Football biography
$12.95 retail

Back to Pass
Choose-your-path
interactive story
$8.95 retail

Save the Season
Choose-your-path
interactive story
$8.95 retail

SOURCES

"About the Trophy." Rimington Trophy Official Site (rimingtontrophy.com). Accessed February 19, 2020.

ACC Digital Network. YouTube (youtube.com).

- "Florida State vs. Michigan Orange Bowl Highlights (2016)." December 30, 2016.
- "Florida State vs. Syracuse Football Highlights (2016)." November 19, 2016.
- "North Carolina vs. Florida State Football Highlights (2016)." October 1, 2016.
- "FSU vs. USF Football Highlights (2016)." September 24, 2016.
- "FSU Legend Warrick Dunn Congratulates Dalvin Cook on Breaking His Record." November 14, 2015.
- "Miami vs. Florida State Football Highlights (2015)." October 10, 2015.
- "Florida State vs. Wake Forest/2015 ACC Football Highlights." October 3, 2015.
- "Florida State vs. South Florida/2015 ACC Football Highlights." September 12, 2015.

"ACL Injury." Mayo Clinic (mayoclinic.org). Accessed February 10, 2020.

Adams, Jonathan. "Florida State vs. Clemson: Score, Stats & Highlights." Heavy (heavy.com). November 7, 2015.

Associated Press. *USA Today* (usatoday.com).

- "Vikings Rookie Dalvin Cook Upbeat About ACL Recovery." November 11, 2017.
- "Florida State's Cook, Miami's Yearby Ex-teammates Now Rivals." October 8, 2015.

Associated Press. "Vikings RB Cook Impressing at Every Stage of ACL Rehab." Fox Sports (fosxports.com). April 24, 2017.

Baily, Stephen. "Florida State Runs Over Syracuse Football in Home Finale." Syracuse.com (syracuse.com). November 19, 2016.

Bair, Scott. "What 49ers Did to Shut Down Dalvin Cook in Playoff Win over Vikings." NBC Sports (nbcsports.com). January 11, 2020.

Baker, Matt. *Tampa Bay Times* (tampabay.com).
- "FSU's Dalvin Cook Snubbed in First Round, Could Go Early on Day 2." April 27, 2017.
- "UNC's Last-Second Field Goal Drops No. 12 Florida State 37-35." October 1, 2016.

Barnes, Craig. "Florida State Wins the 2016 Capital One Orange Bowl." Orange Bowl (orangebowl.org). Accessed January 22, 2020.

Becker, Jon. "Latavius Murray Leaves Raider to Sign with Vikings." *The Mercury News* (mercurynews.com). March 15, 2017.

Bojak. "Miami Central RB Dalvin Cook Named Florida's Mr. Football." Florida Gridiron Preps (floridagridironpreps.com). January 10, 2014.

Bowles, Logan. "Florida State vs. Miami Odds: Canes Favored to Break Streak at 6." SBNation (sbnation.com). October 6, 2016.

Breech, John. "NFL Week 3 Grades: Vikings Get an 'A-' for Blowing Out Raiders, Dolphins Avoid Another 'F'." CBS Sports (cbssports.com). September 23, 2019.

Breeraug, Albert. "Dalvin Cook: The Vikings Rookie Is for Real." *Sports Illustrated* (si.com). August 1, 2017.

Broome, Anthony. "Vikings Blueprint for Successful 2019 Offseason." 247 Sports (247sports.com). January 9, 2019.

Campbell, Dave. Yahoo! Sports (sports.yahoo.com).

- "NFL Rushing Leader Cook Leads Vikes Romp Past Raiders 34-14." September 23, 2019.
- "Cook's 85-Yard TD Highlights Vikings' 20-9 Win vs. Cards." August 24, 2019.

Campbell, Luther. "Telly Lockette Leaving Miami Central High for University of South Florida." *Miami New Times* (miaminewtimes.com). March 5, 2013.

Carlson, Adam. The Viking Age (thevikingage.com).

- "Vikings RB Dalvin Cook Wins Second FedEx Ground Award." October 24, 2019.
- "Dalvin Cook Breaks Minnesota Vikings Rookie Debut Rushing Record." September 12, 2017.
- "Latavius Murray on Minnesota Vikings Naming Dalvin Cook Starter." September 7, 2017.

Chiari, Mike. "Dalvin Cook Breaks Warrick Dunn's FSU Single-Season Rushing Yards Record." Bleacher Report (bleacherreport.com). November 14, 2015.

Clark, Ryan S. "Betty Cook: The Mother of Them All." Warchant (floridastate.rivals.com). September 31, 2016.

Coller, Matthew. "Viking Tidbits: Dalvin Cook Sets a Record, Eric Wilson Fills In, Mike Hughes Returns." SkorNorth (skornorth.com). September 22, 2019.

Conklin, Sean. "Dalvin Cook's First Pro Bowl 'Bittersweet' After Breakout Year." The Patch (patch.com). January 29, 2020.

Connor, Matt. Arrowhead Addict (arrowheadaddict.com).

- "2017 NFL Draft: Dalvin Cook Says He's 'Become a Better Person'." Arrowhead Addict (arrowheadaddict.com). April 12, 2017.
- "NFL Draft Rumors: Could Dalvin Cook Fall Out of the First Round?" March 6, 2017.

Conway, Tyler. Bleacher Report (bleacherreport.com).

- "Dalvin Cook Says He's 'Happy' with Vikings Amid Contract Extension Rumors." January 22, 2020.
- "Dalvin Cook on Return from Knee Surgery: 'It Feels Good. I'm Ready to Go.'" July 30, 2018.

Cooper, Ryan. "New Year's Six Matchups Announced." NCAA (ncaa.com). December 4, 2016.

Cronin, Courtney. ESPN (espn.com).

- "Vikings RB Dalvin Cook Avoids Serious Injury to Shoulder." December 2, 2019.
- "Vikings Sign Veteran Offensive Lineman Kline." March 20, 2019.
- "Dalvin Cook Out for Third Straight Game with Hamstring Injury." October 19, 2018.
- "Dalvin Cook Has Torn ACL, Will Miss Remainder of Rookie Season." October 2, 2017.

Cronin, Courtney and McClure, Vaughn. "Dalvin Cook Has Followed Devonta Freeman's Footsteps—All the Way to Sunday." ESPN (espn.com). September 6, 2019.

Curtis, Charles. "A Guide to Why Dalvin Cook—Potentially the Best RB in the Draft—Fell Out of the First Round." *USA Today* (usatoday.com). April 28, 2017.

Daily Norseman Staff. "2018 NFL Week 17: Chicago Bears at Minnesota Vikings." The Daily Norseman (dailynorseman.com). December 26, 108.

"Dalvin Cook Bio." Alchetron (alchetron.com). Accessed September 29, 2019.

D'Angelo, Tom. "Dalvin Cook Answers Questions about Hamstring with 2 Early TDs." *The Palm Beach Post* (palmbeachpost.com). October 11, 2015.

Deen, Safid.

- "Florida State's Dalvin Cook Will Have to Wait One More Day to Realize His NFL Dream." *The Orlando Sentinel* (orlandosentinel.com). April 27, 2017.
- "FSU Earns New Year's Six Bowl Bid, Will Face Houston in Peach Bowl." *Tallahassee Democrat* (tallahasee.com). December 6, 2015.
- "No. 3 FSU will meet No. 2 Oregon in Rose Bowl." *Tallahassee Democrat* (tallahassee.com). December 7, 2014.
- "Miami Central's Dalvin Cook talks about recruiting, Joseph Yearby, Devonta Freeman, Ermon Lane." Miami Herald High School Sports Blog (miamiherald.typepad.com). December 7, 2013.

Degnan, Susan Miller. "Orange Bowl MVP Dalvin Cook Runs for 145 Yards in FSU Victory, Then Declares for NFL Draft." *Miami Herald* (miamiherald.com). December 31, 2016.

Dibiase, Louie. "An Interview with Roland Smith on Dalvin Cook: He's a Safe Investment." Inside the Iggles (insidetheiggles.com). April 27, 2017.

DiRocco, Michael. "Dalvin Cook 'Willing to Move Forward' from Past Legal Issues." ESPN (espn.com). March 2, 2017.

"Draft Room Call: Dalvin Cook." Minnesota Vikings (vikings.com). Accessed January 19, 2020.

Edholm, Eric. "Vikings-Bears Game in Week 11 Moved to Primetime." Pro Football Weekly (profootballweekly.com). November 5, 2018.

Elliott, Bud. "FSU's Dalvin Cook Has Private Workout with Philadelphia Eagles." Tomahawk Nation (tomahawknation.com). March 29, 2017.

ESPN (espn.com)

- Arizona Cardinals vs. Minnesota Vikings Preseason, Play by Play, August 24, 2019.

- Detroit Lions vs. Minnesota Vikings, Play by Play, October 1, 2017.
- Tampa Bay vs. Minnesota Vikings, Play by Play, September 24, 2017.
- Michigan Wolverines vs. Florida State Seminoles (Orange Bowl), Play by Play. December 30, 2016.
- Florida State Seminoles vs. Syracuse Orange, Play by Play, November 19, 2016.
- North Carolina Tar Heels vs. Florida State Seminoles, Play by Play, October 1, 2016.
- Ole Miss vs. Florida State, Play by Play, September 5, 2016.
- Florida State Seminoles vs. Miami Hurricanes 2014 Play-By-Play. November 15, 2014.

Erby, Glenn. "Report: Vikings RB Dalvin Cook to Miss Game vs. Eagles with Hamstring Injury." The Eagles Wire (theeagleswire.usatoday.com). October 7, 2018.

Fischer, Bryan. "2014 Running Back Dalvin Cook Commits to Clemson." CBS Sports (cbssports.com). June 13, 2012.

Federico Perdomo. "Miami Central vs Gainesville Hurricanes State Final.mp4." YouTube (youtube.com). December 16, 2012.

Fernandez, Andre C. "Miami Central RB Dalvin Cook named Florida's Mr. Football." *Miami Herald* (miamiherald.com). January 10, 2014.

Florida State High School Athletic Association (fhsaa.com).
- "Florida State Championship Game 2013." Accessed October 2, 2019.
- "Florida State Championship Game 2012." Accessed October 2, 2019.

Friedl, Ben. "Derwin James and Dalvin Cook: College Teammates and Friends Go Head-to-Head on Sunday." Los Angeles Chargers (chargers.com). December 12, 2019.

FSU News. "Dalvin Cook Leaves Florida State Its Most Decorated Running Back." App (app.com). December 31, 2016.

Gabriel, Greg. "Why College Pro Days Are Important for NFL Draft Prospects." Bleacher Report (bleacherreport.com). March 6, 2014.

Garcia IV, Bob. "Dalvin Cook Listed as One of Three Rookie Starters for Minnesota." Clutch Points (clutchpoints.com). September 5, 2017.

Graff, Chad. "Dalvin Cook Breaks Adrian Peterson's 3-Game Vikings Rookie Record." *Pioneer Press* (twincities.com). September 24, 2017.

Gray, Jeff. "Florida State RB Devonta Freeman to declare for NFL Draft, per report." SBNation (sbnation.com). January 11, 2014.

Goldkamp, Thomas. "RB Dalvin Cook Flips to Florida." 247 Sports (247sports.com). April 6, 2013.

Heifetz, Danny. "Stefon Diggs Is Mad as Hell. Where Do the Vikings Go from Here?" The Ringer (theringer.com). October 3, 2019.

HeraldHighSchools. "Florida 6A state football final: Miami Central 52, Armwood 7." YouTube (youtube.com). December 14, 2013.

"High School Player Profile: Dalvin Cook." Florida Gridiron Preps (floridagridironpreps.com). Accessed September 30, 2019.

Hoffman, Benjamin. "Vikings Spoil Adrian Peterson's Return with a Tribute to Randy Moss." *The New York Times* (nytimes.com). September 11, 2017.

Hunt, Kelvin. "FSU Football: Writer Questions Dalvin Cook's Character." Fox Sports (foxsports.com). June 30, 2017.

James, Xandria. "Florida State RB Dalvin Cook (ankle) out vs. Syracuse. *Sports Illustrated* (si.com). October 29, 2015.

Johnson, Richard. "What Are the Opening Finals? Explaining Nike's Recruiting Super Bowl in a 2-Minute Read." SBNation (sbnation.com). June 30, 2017.

Judin, Robert. "Dalvin Cook Noncommittal on NFL Draft Decision: 'I Love This University.'" Watch Stadium (watchstadium.com). December 1, 2016.

Jung, Tristan. "Vikings Playoff Odds Take Slight Dive Despite Win Over the Lions in Week 14." Fan Duel (fanduel.com). December 10, 2019.

Kahler, Kalyn. "Bears' Defense Completely Stonewalled Dalvin Cook and the Vikings' Run Game." *Sports Illustrated* (si.com). September 30, 2019.

Krammer, Andrew. "Dalvin Cook's Night in Dallas Earns Him NFC Offensive Player of the Week." *Star Tribune* (startribune.com). November 13, 2019.

Kosnitzky, Adam. "Miami Central Demolishes Palm Bay Heritage." Varsity Preps (varsitypreps.com). December 1, 2013.

Kulha, Andrew. "Florida 5-Star RB Dalvin Cook's Miami Central High School Leads MaxPreps Top 25." Bleacher Report (bleacherreport.com). August 15, 2013.

Linafelt, Tim. "First and 10: Capital One Orange Bowl, Florida State vs. Michigan." Florida State Seminoles (seminoles.com). December 30, 2016.

Long, Corey. "Top Recruits Shine at Under Armour All-America Game." *The Florida Times-Union* (jacksonville.com). January 3, 2014.

Lonien, Luke. "Viking RB Dalvin Cook Continues to Grow at Training Camp." Vikings Wire (vikingswire.usatoday.com). July 25, 2017.

Lyso, Ben. "The Vikings Are on the Verge of an Identity Crisis II: What About Dalvin Cook?" Purple PTSD.com (purpleptsd.com). February 9, 2020.

McCartney, Cory. "Now Florida State's All-Time Leading Rusher, How High Can Dalvin Cook Climb on the ACC List?" Fox Sports (foxsports.com). December 9, 2016.

"Miami Central Teammates Dalvin Cook, Joseph Yearby Primed to Break Out." Athlon Sports (athlonsports.com). June 17, 2015.

Mizutani, Dane. "Cook Excited to Face Former Mentor." *Duluth News Tribune* (duluthnewstribune.com). September 5, 2019.

Murphy, Brian. "Rehabbing Viking RB Dalvin Cook: 'I'm still that same guy.'" *The Daily Republic* (mitchellrepublic.com). June 5, 2018.

Nanvati, Rajan. "Dalvin Cook: The NFL's Most Underdiscussed Superstar." Medium (medium.com). November 15, 2019.

NBC. "2017 NFL Draft Profile: Florida State RB Dalvin Cook." NBC Sports (nbcsports.com). April 5, 2017.

Nelson, Joe. *Bring Me the News* (bringmethenews.com).

- "Dalvin Cook Leads All Running Backs in Pro Bowl Voting." December 16, 2019.
- "We Asked Dalvin Cook's HS Coach About His Chances in the NFL." May 10, 2017.

Newberg, Josh. "Dalvin Cook vs. Joseph Yearby." 247 Sports (247sports.com). November 12,2014.

NFL. YouTube (youtube.com).

- "Dalvin Cook Takes It 85 Yds to the House!" August 24, 2019.
- "Lions vs. Bears Week 10 Highlights/NFL 2018." November 11, 2018.
- "Lions vs. Vikings Week 9 Highlights/NFL 2018." November 4, 2018.
- "Dalvin Cook Highlights vs. Tampa Bay/Buccaneers vs. Vikings/Wk 3 Player Highlights." September 24, 2017.

NFL (nfl.com).

- "FedEx Air & Ground Players 2019." Accessed February 21, 2020.
- "NFL Reveals Rosters for 2020 Pro Bowl in Orlando." December 17, 2019.

"NFL Draft Tracker 2017." SBNation (sbnation.com). Accessed February 1, 2020.

OddsShark. SBNation (sbnation.com).

- "Houston vs. Florida State Odds, Peach Bowl 2015: Seminoles Betting Favorite vs. Cougars." December 28, 2015.
- "The Oregon Ducks Enter the Rose Bowl as Big Favorites over Florida State." December 19, 2014.

"Orange Bowl History – the 2010's." Orange Bowl (orangebowl.org). Accessed January 21, 2020.

Panacy, Peter. Niner Noise (ninernoise.com).

- "49ers No. 1 Priority vs. Vikings Should be Stopping Dalvin Cook." Niner Noise (ninernoise.com). January 7, 2020.
- "49ers vs. Rams: Don't Expect Los Angeles to Rest Starters in Week 17." December 26, 2018.

Parsons, Kelly. "Times' Blue-Chip Player of Year: Miami Central's Dalvin Cook." *Tampa Bay Times* (tampabay.com). January 26, 2014.

Patrick, Adam. The Viking Age (thevikingage.com).

- "Vikings Players, Rest of NFC Fall Short in 2020 Pro Bowl." January 26, 2020.
- "5 Takeaways from the Vikings Week 4 Loss to the Bears." September 30, 2019.
- "Adrian Peterson Has a Specific Goal in Mind for Next Week's Vikings Game." September 4, 2017.
- "Minnesota Vikings Announce Official Dates for 2017 Training Camp." June 16, 2017.

Perez, Bryan. "Experts Split Over Bears vs. Vikings Week 11 Matchup." Bears Wire (bearswire.usatoday.com). November 16, 2018.

Pickman, Ben. "Vikings' Dalvin Cook Exits vs. Seahawks with Shoulder Injury." *Sports Illustrated* (si.com). December 2, 2019.

Polacek, Scott. "Dalvin Cook Ruled Out vs. Bills with Hamstring Injury." Bleacher Report (bleacherreport.com). September 21, 2018.

"Pretrial Intervention Law and Legal Definition." U.S. Legal (uslegal.com). Accessed October 7, 2019.

Pro Football Reference (pro-football-reference.com).

- Adrian Peterson Bio. Accessed March 23, 2020.
- Dalvin Cook Pro Bio. Accessed December 17, 2019.
- Ted Brown Pro Bio. Accessed January 11, 2020.
- Warrick Dunn Bio. Accessed January 13, 2020.

Ragatz, Will. *Sports Illustrated* (si.com).

- "Dalvin Cook Is on a Historic Pace Through Ten Games in 2019." November 11, 2019.
- "Dalvin Cook Voted FedEx Ground Player of the Week." September 17, 2019.

Rand, Michael. "Blazing Fast Vikings RB Dalvin Cook Shows How Irrelevant 40-yard Dash Times Can Be." *Star Tribune* (startribune.com). September 13, 2017.

Rapaport, Daniel. "Sam Bradford Says His Knee Injury Not from Contact." *Sports Illustrated* (si.com). September 20, 2017.

Rapp, Timothy. "Dalvin Cook Says Hamstring Injury Isn't 100 Percent: 'I'm Just Not There Yet.'" Bleacher Report (bleacherreport.com). October 1, 2018.

Reedy, Joe. "No. 20 Florida State Starts Fast in Rout of Boston College." Associated Press (apnews.com). November 11, 2016.

Reidell, Robert. "Vikings Draft Picks 2017: Results, Grades and Analysis for Each Selection." Bleacher Report (bleacherreport.com). April 27, 2017.

Robbins, Joe. "FSU's Dalvin Cook Is Fast Moving, Soft-spoken—and Arguably the Most Talented Running Back in the Nation." *Sports Illustrated* (si.com). March 10, 2016.

Roberson, Doug. "Houston Corrals FSU's Dalvin Cook." *The Atlanta Journal-Constitution* (ajc.com). December 31, 2015.

Rollins, Khadrice. "Vikings Coach Mike Zimmer Confirmed Rookie Running Back Dalvin Cook Has a Torn ACL." *Sports Illustrated* (si.com). October 2, 2017.

Rosvoglou, Chris. "Injury Update on Minnesota Vikings Star RB Dalvin Cook." The Spun (thespun.com). November 8, 2019.

Sampson, Brian. "Green Bay Packers vs Minnesota Vikings: Keys to Victory in Week 2." The Dairyland Express (dairlyandexpress.com). September 15, 2019.

Sansavere, Bob. "Dalvin Cook Reminds Vikings How Much Better They Are with Him on the Field." *Pioneer Press* (twincities.com). November 4, 2018.

Schlabach, Mark. "Dalvin Cook named in police report." ESPN (espn.com). December 24, 2014.

Schmidt, Matthew. "Why Vikings RB Dalvin Cook Is in for Another Huge Performance Against the Raiders." Clutch Points (clutchpoints.com). September 20, 2019.

Scott, Jelani. "Vikings RB Dalvin Cook Injures Clavicle in 'MNF' Loss." NFL (nfl.com). December 2, 2019.

Shanker, Jared. "FSU's Dalvin Cook to Miss Time After Having Shoulder Surgery." ESPN (espn.com). April 6, 2016.

Shipley, John. "No More Injury Talk for Vikings' Dalvin Cook. 'I'm Good,' He Says." *West Central Tribune* (wctrib.com). January 7, 2020.

SI Wire. "Dalvin Cook Apparently the Victim of Sabotage Campaign." *Sports Illustrated* (si.com). April 25, 2017.

Smalls II, C. Isaiah. "Without Devonta Freeman, There May Be No Dalvin Cook. Now the Miami Natives Face Off." *Miami Herald* (miamiherald.com). September 5, 2019.

Smith, Eric. Minnesota Vikings (vikings.com).
- "Vikings Secure Postseason Berth with Rams Loss." December 21, 2019.
- "Dalvin Cook a Difference Maker in Postseason Debut." January 5, 2019.
- "Vikings Fortify Offensive Line with Addition of Josh Kline." March 20, 2019.
- "Notebook: Dalvin Cook 'Hyped' for Vikings Playoff Chase." November 15, 2018.

Sonnone, Brendan. "Report: Saboteur Tried to Sink FSU RB Dalvin Cook's Draft Stock." 247 Sports (247sports.com). April 25, 2017.

"Spielman: 45-Minute Phone Conversation with Cook Sealed Vikings' Decision to Draft Him." SiriusXM (siriusxm.com). May 1, 2017.

Sports Reference (sports-reference.com)

- Dalvin Cook College Bio. Accessed December 17, 2019.
- Michigan vs. Florida State (Orange Bowl). December 30, 2016.
- Florida vs. Florida State. November 26, 2016.
- Florida State vs. Syracuse. November 19, 2016.
- Boston College vs. Florida State. November 11, 2016.
- Florida State vs. North Carolina State. November 5, 2016.
- Clemson vs. Florida State. October 29, 2016.
- Wake Forest vs. Florida State. October 15, 2016.
- Florida State vs. Miami Hurricanes. October 8, 2016.
- North Carolina vs. Florida State. October 1, 2016.
- Florida State vs. South Florida. September 24, 2016.
- Florida State vs. Louisville. September 17, 2016.
- Charleston Southern vs. Florida State. September 10, 2016.
- Houston vs. Florida State, Peach Bowl. December 31, 2015.
- Florida State vs. Florida. November 28, 2015.
- Chattanooga vs. Florida State. November 21, 2015.
- North Carolina State vs. Florida State. November 14, 2015.
- Florida State vs. Clemson. November 7, 2015.
- Syracuse vs. Florida State. October 31, 2015.
- Florida State vs. Georgia Tech. October 24, 2015.
- Louisville vs. Florida State. October 17, 2015.
- Miami vs. Florida State. October 10, 2015.
- Florida State vs. Wake Forest. October 3, 2015.
- Florida State vs. Boston College. September 18, 2015.
- South Florida vs. Florida State. September 12, 2015.
- Texas State vs. Florida State. September 5, 2015.

Taylor, John. "FSU's Dalvin Cook Cited Last Year for Chaining Three Puppies Together." NBC Sports (collegefootballtalk.nbcsports.com). July 12, 2015.

Team BCP. "Miami Central Rockets Might Lose 2011 Wins." Big Country Preps (bigcountrypreps.com). August 13, 2012.

"This Day in History, June 8, 1966: NFL and AFL Announce Merger." The History Channel (history.com). Accessed February 12, 2020.

Thompson, Eric J. The Daily Norseman (dailynorseman.com).
- "Vikings vs. Bears Week 17: Five Game-Changing Plays." December 31, 2018.
- "Vikings at Bears Week 11: Five Game-Changing Plays." November 19, 2018.

Todoroff, Eric. "It's Official: Cook, Walker Named Consensus All-Americans by NCAA." Florida State Seminoles (seminoles.com). December 15, 2016.

Tomasson, Chris. *Pioneer Press* (twincities.com).
- "Vikings RB Dalvin Cook Said He Felt 'Good' in Return from Hamstring Injury." September 27, 2018.
- "Vikings RB Dalvin Cook Undergoes Successful ACL Surgery." October 10, 2017.

Town-Crier Editor. "Stars Shine at Heath Evans Foundation Tourney." *Go Town Crier* (gotowncrier.com). June 22, 2012.

Vensel, Matt. "Vikings Do Due Draft Diligence to Grab Dalvin Cook." *Star Tribune* (startribune.com). April 29, 2017.

Villani, Jared. "Report: Kevin Sefanski to Return as Vikings' Full-Time Offensive Coordinator." Clutch Points (clutchpoints.com). January 9, 2019.

"What Is a Torn Shoulder Labrum?" Healthline (healthline.com). Accessed January 13, 2020.

Williams, Charean. "Dalvin Cook Misses Practice with Hamstring Injury." Pro Football Talk (profootballtalk.nbcsports.com). October 3, 2018.

Wludford. The Daily Norseman (dailynorseman.com).

- "Dalvin Cook: He Can Shine—But Can He Stay on the Field?" May 24, 2019.
- "A Closer Look at Dalvin Cook." May 1, 2017.

Young, Lindsey. "Dalvin Cook: Shoulder Injury 'Not the End of the World.'" Minnesota Vikings (vikings.com). December 19, 2019.

Yotter, Tim. "Hughes on Mend from ACL Surgery, Receiving Tips from Cook." 247 Sports (247sports.com). December 28, 2018.

Zone Coverage. "9/8/19: Dalvin Cook on Postgame Jersey Exchange with Devonta Freeman." YouTube (youtube.com). September 8, 2019.

Zucker, Joseph. "Dalvin Cook Injury: Updates on FSU Star's Hamstring and Return." Bleacher Report (bleacherreport.com). October 5, 2015.

ABOUT THE AUTHOR

Doug Olson, Jr., holds a degree in journalism from the University of Minnesota. He has contributed several pieces of fiction and nonfiction to various publications, including some comic book work.

A storyteller by nature, Doug spent countless hours regaling neighborhood kids with tales of ghosts, superheroes, and *The Six-Million Dollar Man* "fan fiction," before such a thing existed. He has continued his love of wordsmithing throughout his life, even when he knows it may never be seen by another human being.

Doug enjoys creating, brainstorming with friends, playing *World of Warcraft*, and, of course, following his beloved Minnesota Vikings. He lives in the Minneapolis area with his wife, two children, and four small fur-babies.

Made in the USA
Monee, IL
01 December 2020

50475099R00066